Dedicated to all who have felt curved and bent in some way.
Look to that heart part of you where love begins and spirit
lives... And you will find your own unique way to shine.

Author: Katherine Stephens
Illustrator: Lisa McNamara
Editors: Rachyl Stone and Diane Alexander

Twink the Starfish has a special message for you...

This is a story about purpose, meaning and magic. It is about feeling like you are different...that you are not the same as everyone else. It is also about the gifts we are given and how we are more than we think we are.
It's a story about LIFE.

Let's go back to the beginning...

As far back as I can remember, I felt uncomfortable about the way I looked. I felt I wasn't like most of the other starfish. They all had long, straight arms. They could swim so fast, play games and do it all without any problems.

I could play too, but it just took me longer because one of my arms was curved and bent around.

Sometimes the other sea creatures made fun of me.

Grandma Star was always kind and loving. She would whisper to me, "Pay them no mind Twink, dear...because you are special and unique in your own way and someday they will see just how special you are!
I have a feeling you will make someone very happy, just by being YOU."

"How could I make someone happy Grandma Star?" She smiled a knowing smile, pulled me close, patted my little spiny head, and said, "Just wait little one, you'll see; being different can be a special blessing...even a precious gift."

"How can that be? I asked?" "Because you carry an important message."

"I have a message? What could it be? I'm so little, what difference could I possibly make?"

"Trust me," she said knowingly, "you will make a difference. Just wait and see! Now run along and we'll visit more next time."

The reassuring words Grandma Star said made me feel better; but the ugly comments others made to me, still hurt my feelings. I clung to her words in hopes that someday I would understand why I was different.

That night as I dropped off to sleep, I tried to imagine what wondrous adventures lay before me...a little starfish with a bent and curved arm.

Many tides had come and gone until one day I found myself lying on the beach basking in the sun; warming myself and enjoying the sounds of children playing in the ocean nearby.

All of a sudden a lady stopped, bent over and picked me up. She paused for a very long time as she carefully examined me. She held me so gently, and lovingly. It was as if I was precious to her and you know what?

I WAS!

As the lady looked at me, she too saw that one of my arms was bent and curved. To her that made me special, beautiful and unique. For in my appearance she found a precious gift...a meaning and purpose to something that had happened in her life.

She had been very ill and her illness caused her body to change. This change affected the way she felt about herself until she found me. My special appearance reassured her of her own inner beauty. I was no less a starfish because my arm was curved and bent, and she was no less a woman because her body had changed.

We both rejoiced! I had finally found my destiny. I brought hope, happiness, and insight to someone! She found a new sense of self-assurance, confidence and meaning; both of us special and different---wonderfully, uniquely different.

Grandma Star was right! We are more than our perceived limitations. We all have a wonderful ability to be all that we are meant to be. This gift is ours alone to share. What someone might see as flaws, obstacles or challenges; another will see as a blessing - a special gift.

Now I know what it means to be uniquely me!

No Less A Starfish

Altered and different I may appear to be. Not the same as most of the starfish you see. But in my heart I know the real me, special and loving–Uniquely me.

The message is simple and very clear. It's the inside you that matters most. So don't be afraid, embarrassed or shy; For each of us is blessed by a power divine, to find our own individual way to shine.

Remember that special place within, where your heart lives and love begins. Gift others with kindness and thoughtful care.
No matter your problems, they'll soon disappear.

You're no less perfect than imperfect me. It's the heart that counts...
Love + One = Uniquely you and uniquely me.

~Katherine Stephens

Notes

Can you find:

pillow, wheel, anchor, puff fish, bottle, snail, crab, turtle, seashell, eyeglasses, telescope

Made in the USA
Middletown, DE
30 June 2020